IF YOU'RE A DUFFER, YOU'RE OK IN MY BOOK

IF YOU'RE A DUFFER, YOU'RE OK IN MY BOOK

Getting the Most Out of a Round, Even If You'll Never Break 80 or 90

By Mike Pavlik

Foreword by Rockmond Dunbar

Skyhorse Publishing

Skyhorse Publishing books may be purchased in bulk at special discounts for sales promotion, corporate gifts, fund-raising, or educational purposes. Special editions can also be created to specifications. For details, contact the Special Sales Department, Skyhorse Publishing, 307 West 36th Street, 11th Floor, New York, NY 10018 or info@skyhorsepublishing.com.

Skyhorse® and Skyhorse Publishing® are registered trademarks of Skyhorse Publishing, Inc.®, a Delaware corporation.
Visit our website at www.skyhorsepublishing.com.

10 9 8 7 6 5 4 3 2 1

Library of Congress Cataloging-in-Publication Data is available on file.

Cover design by Owen Corrigan
Cover photo credit Thinkstock

ISBN: 978-1-63220-493-6
Ebook ISBN 978-1-63220-863-7

Printed in the United States of America

Dedication

To my sons, Stephen and Jason, and to all golfers who simply enjoy playing the game of golf.

Acknowledgments

I would like to thank Editor Judy Thompson and Graphic Artist Jason Pavlik for all their assistance.

Foreword
by Rockmond Dunbar

As an actor, in a career where big bucks are spent on making the imaginary, real, and where the mantra "fake it 'til you make it," was born, it came as a genuine shock to realize that not only was I terrible at acting like I was a great golfer, but even worse, I was actually a certifiably terrible golfer. Let me tell you, the game of golf—and it is a game after all—didn't become truly enjoyable to me until I identified my skill set and accepted it as such. My name is Rockmond Dunbar, and I am a DUFFER. There, I said it. Initially, embracing the reality that I was by no means, in this life, ever going to be near the level of Tiger Woods, or Sergio Garcia, was difficult.

I mean, come on, I had all of the right "stuff," right? I had the best clubs, shoes, all the gadgets, and top-of-the-line gear. If I couldn't play like the big boys, I would at least look like them—until I actually had to start playing, which is where things would always get a little tricky. What would start off as a relaxing day on the green would end with me feeling more worked up and frustrated than when I started. And everyone knows, even a duffer, that the last thing you should feel at the end of a game of golf is worse. I'm pretty certain it's against the unwritten "laws of the game." I needed to find my way back to loving the sport that I was never too great at, but determined to enjoy. This is where Mike's **If You're A Duffer, You're OK in My Book** came to the rescue.

Wrought with humor and invaluable lessons, this book takes the pain out of expanding one's golf set, and instead, replaces it with all of the helpful tools necessary in growing one's abilities and techniques in the game. Written with the everyday "duffer" in mind, each section breaks down the essentials, while flowing seamlessly into the next lesson. Mike's ability to simplify what is many times a difficult process in becoming a better golfer allows the reader to get lost in the fun of the game, instead of the technicality of it all. In the end, that's what it's all about anyway, right? A whole lot of fun with growth in your game along the way—that's all a duffer can ask for, and that's everything that Mike Pavlik gives in this gem of a book.

CONTENTS

IF YOU'RE A DUFFER, YOU'RE OK IN MY BOOK

SECTION 1

- ➢ Duffer Introduction
- ➢ Duffer History
- ➢ Duffer Definitions
- ➢ Duffer Essentials

Duffer Introduction

I wrote this book for the golfer who just enjoys getting out with the guys once or twice a week—the golfer who takes pleasure in a round carding one or two pars, a few bogeys, a few double bogeys, and once in a while that nasty 8, even after using the mulligan. Of course, these are scores that are sometimes caused by that hazardous journey through sand and water along the way. Your average 9-hole round falls within the 46 to 54 range, but you still feel good based on the few good shots you remember—this is what keeps you coming back.

Sometimes there are extraneous factors that affect your game. You might play with guys who prefer early tee times; you like late ones. It might take you a few strokes to warm up to the course while your buddies are familiar with the territory, but after a few hits you're up to speed. And there is always the long hitter, impressing us by his distance, which sometimes energizes you to swing harder than usual with the reverse effect. Once in a while you need to use the restroom on the course and when you turn on the faucet to wash your hands, the water splashes all over the front of you. You know what it looks like and what your buddies might think—maybe next time it will happen to them.

For duffers, the par 3 holes are nice; they put you on an equal basis with the group. You need to view each shot as a new chance, although sometimes it's hard to shake off the bad ones. You might find if you don't overthink the shot, you do much better. You should learn to take what the club gives you and move on. Naturally, this all sounds good; I only wish I could do it, but perhaps I am not maximizing the use of my resources.

I am retired and live in Arizona, where I could practice daily, year round. Nearby there's a chipping course, sand trap area, and a driving range, if I wanted to take the time to practice, but I don't. Practice takes the fun out of the game and turns it into work. Instead, I watch golf on TV, read my golf magazines, browse the golf stores, check the email golf ads, and play a round once or twice a week.

I exercise each morning to stay limber. My routine consists of waist twists, arm rotations, pushups, elastic band curls, and touching toes—or as far below my knees as I can stretch. The number of repetitions I do for each exercise corresponds to my age, so I only have to improve by one repetition each year.

I live in a golf community but haven't purchased a club membership. I don't even have a golf cart for my golf cart garage; I can't justify one since I only play six times a year on my home course. I prefer to play a variety of courses. There are 131 courses in the area, and I'm still looking for the one on which I play the best. Playing on different courses does give me one thing—an excuse for being over par since I'm not familiar with the course.

I have tried different golf balls, and for now I prefer a ball that has a clear plastic coating; they work best for me in distance and putting. My golfing buddies don't use this style of ball, so mine is easy to find on the course—sometimes accompanied by their chuckling because of where the ball is found.

I do have a Golf GPS unit I take with me, when I remember to charge it. I use it to aid me in club selection, and I don't have to hunt the fairway markers. I have a good estimate of my individual club distance, with minimal overlap. The overlap occurs since I carry a few extra clubs; one day the golf police will get me.

My biggest problem is direction. I know where I want the ball to go, but I can't always deliver. You may find that opening the club face, not lining up correctly, pulling the club inward, trying to kill the ball, overthinking the shot, and the closeness of sand or water adversely affect the shot. I know this but it takes work to correct.

In my group of golfers, I have the highest handicap; someone has to. It used to bother me, but as long as I play the best I can, there is not much else to do. I have good days and bad, just like all golfers. Based on my handicap I also get more strokes for the skins game we play each round, which is the upside of being bad.

In my golf history, I've had an ace, eagle, birdie, par, bogey, double bogey, triple bogey, and quadruple bogey. I use my mulligan faithfully, when I remember. If I put my best holes together into one fantasy round, I would post a 25 and 27, for a 52! Not bad for a duffer—justification for continuing my play in the quest for improvement.

Later in this book I share a round of my golf with you. You would think I would pick my best round to use in this book. Rather, I just picked the next course I played. I had played this course before and was hoping for a good score. Needless to say, I had a not-so-good round. That's the way my golf game goes—always in need of improvement.

I often wonder how much you would have to spend to buy every product advertised to improve your game. The only ones I would consider purchasing are those that don't require work.

My goal is to strike each shot to the best of my ability and play the next shot as a challenge wherever it happens to be. I believe we all think a good game with a plan on what we would like each shot to do, but it doesn't always turn out that way.

I would like to keep my score in the 90s and improve. However, I usually have one or two holes that seem beyond my control. I know what I'm trying to do with my shots, but sometimes I don't hit the shot I planned.

I see potential, so I try to accent the positive and enjoy my good shots—and the once-in-a-while exceptional shot.

I compiled this book to let you guys, who play like I do, know it's alright to be a duffer. Be honest evaluating your attitude and game later in this book using my observations and checklists to determine if you are on par with the duffer.

Duffer History

I first tried to play the game of golf while in high school in the early 1960s. I lived in Ohio, where there was a yearly six-month window to play golf, as long as it didn't rain. I started by using my dad's clubs; he had not played in a while, and they were just sitting there. The first rounds were with my buddies who were starting also, so we hacked around the courses. Did we practice? No. Our method was to play our regular rounds on the course as practice. I guess once you form a habit, you stick with it. My scores were in the 60s, much like the times, filled with peace, love, and war. I played maybe ten times.

Returning home after my freshman year of college I asked my dad if I could take the clubs back with me, as I had found some friends who played once in a while. At this time, my dad's work was seasonal, and he didn't have time to play golf. He said it was OK. However, I did receive an objection from my older brother, who also wanted to use the clubs. I was unaware he played golf, but we decided on how to settle the problem. We felt the only "fair way" to settle this was via a golf match, with the winner getting the use of the clubs. The match was close, as I remember it (45 years ago)—about one or two strokes separated us. I was victorious.

The college years didn't afford much time to play golf, although the university did have a reasonably priced course. It was the late 1960s, and momentous things were going on in our country. It was hard to be taken seriously in golf clothes with a golf bag. I remember playing a few times but not any memorable rounds.

After college, I accepted a position as an art teacher in my home town. A lot of my college friends lived in the area, and we began an annual golf outing reunion. The golf course we played was operated by a friend's family in Hinckley, Ohio, where the buzzards return annually, but I could find no birdies on the course.

I was able to return "my" clubs to my dad when I got a new set of clubs for my thirtieth birthday. For the next twenty years I still only played about ten rounds a year. I was also able to get my dad out a few times. I didn't buy any new clubs because mine were hardly used. Needless to say, my game did not change or improve.

Upon retirement from teaching (after 35 years), my wife and I relocated to Arizona. We built a home in a senior community with five golf courses. I try to get out twice a week for most of the year and only weekly during the high-priced winter season when the snowbirds return.

Upon our relocation, I felt I should replace my clubs with something new. I started looking through golf magazines and watching the ads on the Golf Channel to help with my decision. For my irons, I selected a set of Controller irons that stated they would correct any errant shots by their roll and bulge design. On the Internet, I ordered a long-distance driver, an Xplosion oversize driver. Surprisingly, I found a club I liked and could hit. The only errors were my fault. I then added a 3 metal fairway wood, which seems to work well most of the time. From a catalog, I added the 5, 7, and 9, fairway metal woods, which helped once I was able to get the distances down. To accommodate them, I removed the 4 iron from my bag. I added a chipper for the close shots. And lastly, I found a short putter that works for me.

Although I carry sixteen clubs in my bag, I have never been questioned by the bag police. I keep the extra clubs in case a special need arises. If I had to, I could eliminate the 3 iron and the escape wedge. But until I get cited, I will keep them in my bag.

I try to use a high-quality golf ball that is different from what the guys in my group use. I find the clear-coated balls work the best, and I don't have to mark them. They are reasonably priced and last a number of rounds before I lose them.

Even with the upgraded equipment, my game really hasn't changed. I still shoot in my range (46–54) on a standard course. Like most players, I have good days and bad days. I try to increase my positives each round.

My best round ever was a score of 37 on a par 36 front nine of a round. I had 5 pars, 2 birdies, 1 bogey, and 1 double bogey. It was really a great feeling. However, it didn't carry over to the back nine, as I had only one par and carded a 47. Ultimately, it was still one of my lowest 18-hole rounds ever. FYI, I was 62 and freshly retired.

It's not a disgrace to be a duffer. As a happy duffer, you know your skills and limitations and try to improve your game each time out.

Duffer Definitions

Golf—A game played on a challenging course in which the object is to drive a ball into a series of holes (9 or 18) in the fewest number of strokes.

Ace—Hole in one. To hit the ball from the tee into the cup in one stroke. A duffer's dream.

Par—A score for each hole based on the distance and two putts on the green for a ball to go from the tee to the cup. Attainable occasionally by a duffer on a few holes in a good round.

Birdie—A score on a hole of one under par. A duffer may have a look at a birdie once in a while and occasionally may make one.

Eagle—A score on a hole of two under par. A rare bird for most golfers.

Double Eagle—A score on a hole of three under par (i.e., 2 on a par 5). A rare shot for any golfer.

Bogey—A score on a hole of one over par. Usually accompanied by the comment "it should have gone in."

Double Bogey—A score on a hole of two over par. Usually accompanied by the comment "damn that was close."

Triple Bogey—A score on a hole of three over par. Usually accompanied by a comment about the water or sand or both that came into play on that hole.

Quadruple Bogey—A score on a hole of 4 over par. A duffer can accept this because a professional golfer shot this on a televised tournament. Followed by the comment "thank goodness that hole is over."

Tee—The starting area for a hole of golf. A small peg used to elevate a golf ball.

Teed off—Having hit the ball from the tee. Mood caused by a bad shot from the tee.

Drive—Move forcibly as to hit a ball off the tee.

Whiff—A slight current or gust of air created by missing the ball while trying to hit it. The result of an overactive shot attempt trying to hit the ball farther than you know you can.

Mulligan—A second chance to correct an errant shot with no penalty by replaying the shot. A do-over. A possible redemption.

Gimme—(Also 'pick it up.') Having a short putt on the green conceded by a member of your golfing group. Music to a duffer's ears.

Foot Wedgie—Kicking the ball from a bad landing spot to a better location to hit it. Unacceptable, even by a duffer.

Provisional—Having hit the tee shot into a location where the ball may not be found, or hitting it possibly out of bounds, and having no mulligan left, a second ball is hit from the tee to be played if the first ball is not found or is indeed out of bounds. This keeps the game moving, since you would have to go back to the tee to re-hit after searching for your ball and not finding it or finding it out of bounds. It would count as your third stroke if used.

Duffing—A description or recounting by a duffer.

Duffer Essentials

1. Balls

There are many golf balls on the market with great and amazing claims and prices to match. Some need to be fitted to your swing and speed, others have various dimple patterns and constructions, and all come in a multitude of colors.

When I started playing more often, I used a ball that was different from that of my playing partners. This made it easier to distinguish my ball near other balls, although that didn't happen often.

The first ball I chose was discontinued about a year after I started using it. This was the ball I used to get my one and only eagle.

The ball I chose as a replacement became unavailable locally and on the Internet after three years. Upon contacting the company, I was told that they didn't manufacture them anymore, and they sent me a dozen of their new balls. The second ball I couldn't get any more is the one I used to get my one and only hole in one.

My third and current ball of choice is a construction style and not a brand. I prefer the clear-coated golf balls in a variety of colors. These balls fly the best for me, very seldom mark, and putt very smoothly. Since I don't have a specific brand, I usually buy them in bulk quantities at various golf expos.

2. Tees

I feel each golfer should try and decide what size tee best suits their style and swing.

I began using the basic large tee of $2\frac{3}{4}$ inches, but my drives were low and scattered, and I often topped the ball.

I checked the golf stores to see what was available and experimented with various sizes. I determined the best size for my golf style and swing was the $3\frac{1}{4}$-inch tee. I could get into the different composite tees, but I chose the simple wood ones. My drives are now loftier and farther. Either tee up or get teed off.

3. Clubs

My clubs are a mixture of various brands that I have accumulated and that work for me—at given times. I watch the commercials on Golf Channel showing all the aids and equipment needed be the state-of-the-art golfer. I do get tempted to test some, but that thought quickly passes.

I also realize the limitations of my game and equipment. I know what my clubs can do and I am confident in that knowledge. The only variable is me.

I can shank it, pull it, rip it, top it, yank it, turn it, yip it, whiff it, and once in a while get that sweet shot. I learned not to throw the club or beat it into the ground, since it is not the fault of the club, ball, or tee.

My basic bag holds irons 3, 5, 6, 7, 8, 9, PW, SW, and an escape wedge. My driver and 3, 5, 7, and 9 hybrids complete my legal bag. The last addition to my bag is an approach chipper and a putter.

Finding a putter was difficult. I tend to bend over my putts to the extent that I want my eyes directly over the ball. On previous putters, when I bent over my ball, my hands were on the shaft. This was not very comfortable and not a good feel. I searched golf stores until I found a very short one (perhaps designed for a youth) that was exactly what I wanted. The putter is 29 inches high, so short that I can't lean on it when I am on the green. My golfing buddies still tend to make fun of it or of me.

If you added up my clubs, you would know that I bag sixteen clubs. I rationalize that I very rarely use some of my clubs, and if I need to get down to the legal fourteen, I would drop the escape wedge and the 3 iron. But until the golf police cite me . . .

Using my mismatched, over-the-legal-limit number of clubs, I was able to record a personal best round of 84. Unfortunately, I have only been able to come close a few times since then.

4. GPS

This unit speeds up the pace of the game and hastens club selection by providing the distance to hazards and the pin. It beats asking your partner: "How far is the green?" since your guess is as good as his.

5. Golf Glove

I use a basic golf glove from an online source. I don't really need it, but it makes me look like I know what I'm doing. I keep the glove on the whole round except for the pit stops; it's hard to wash your hands with a glove on. I've noticed some golfers remove their glove to chip or putt. Since I don't know why, I will continue to keep my glove on.

I also have a pair of winter golfing gloves. It really does get cold in the mornings in the Arizona desert.

6. Golf Discount Cards

There are numerous golf cards available, which provide easy booking and discount rates at many courses. Some also provide incentives such as free products or discounts at golf stores. The cards give you the freedom to play a variety of courses.

7. Golf Magazines

I don't subscribe to any golf magazines but receive a few monthly publications as a perk from the purchase of my golf discount cards. I look at the game improvement sections and have tried a few corrections that do work. The problem is that each magazine offers different teachers with various solutions or equipment "guaranteed" to solve the same problem. I prefer to aim, hit it, and take what I get.

8. Duffer Golf Course

I propose a small change to existing golf facilities to create a duffer golf course. Any golf course can be slightly modified and designed to accommodate the over-average golfer, the once in a while golfer, the seasonal golfer, and the golfer who doesn't want any undue pressure. The course is modified to offset the occasional bad hole a golfer may experience and not spoil the round.

All that needs to be done is add a short par 4 leading up to the original first tee. This would be hole 19. (Another solution is for the duffer to play the first hole twice and record both scores.) Each duffer would play and record scores on all 19 holes and then discard the score of the worst hole of the day for his "official" score on the round. Non-duffers would use 19 as a warm-up hole.

This concept of the extra hole allows for the possible removal of tension and pressure the duffer feels at the clubhouse or first tee.

9. Duffer Adjustment (any course)

Each golfer would be granted mulligans based on their average scores.

Those with scores:

In the 80s – one mulligan
In the 90s – two mulligans
In the 100s – three mulligans

To be used as needed. If unused at the end of the round, the mulligans would be subtracted from the final score.

SECTION 2

- ➢ Preface
- ➢ Duffer Description
- ➢ Duffer Ideals
- ➢ Duffer Observations
- ➢ Duffer Experiences
- ➢ Duffer Expressions

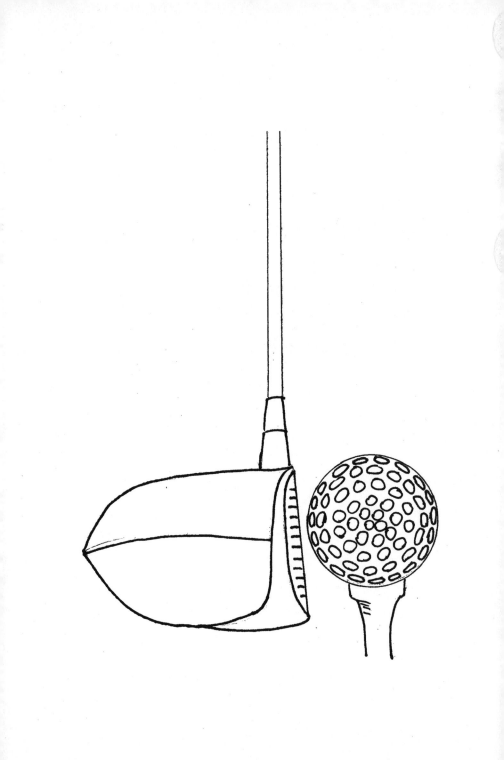

Preface

This section consists of golf concepts presented that encompass these areas:

- ➤ Duffer Description
- ➤ Duffer Ideals
- ➤ Duffer Observations
- ➤ Duffer Experiences
- ➤ Duffer Expressions

Grab your golf pencil, sit back, relax, and mark your responses to each of the following checklists, indicating points that apply to your golfing.

After completing these checklists, you will determine if you're OK in my book.

Tee up, turn the page, and begin!

Duffer Description

To use the word "duffer" as descriptive of my golfing, I thought I would look up the meaning of the term. I had a copy of *The New American Webster Handy College Dictionary* available, which gave me the following definition:

"A stupid or inefficient person; a poor player at a game."

After reading this, I figured Noah never played golf.

I was slightly offended and would not accept this as a true description of the term as applied to a golfer. So a redefinition was necessary.

Now is the time to grab your pencil and mark those descriptions I have listed that apply to you.

My new definition follows:

A golf duffer is a player who

____ tries to the best of his ability but lacks the skills of a professional

____ performs with an average degree of skill, enjoys playing the game, and tries to improve their ability

____ takes enjoyment in his good shots and is annoyed by his errant shots but continues to play because he is optimistic that more good shots are coming

____ takes encouragement while watching a pro tournament and observing a player making a bogey, knowing he can do that, too

____ occasionally buys new equipment "guaranteed" to reduce strokes

____ is courteous to other golfers and acknowledges good play

_____ can't create backspin or shape a shot to the green

_____ enjoys and respects the game of golf

_____ tries to the best of his abilities to play the game as it should be played

_____ takes satisfaction in the few quality shots struck in a round

_____ appreciates the good shots (efforts) of his fellow golfers

_____ can say "good shot" and mean it

_____ appreciates a "gimme"

_____ feels undue pressure at a water hazard or drop zone

_____ "reads" the green and doesn't understand why the ball breaks the other way

_____ might often carry more than fourteen clubs in the bag

_____ doesn't get mad when he loses a ball (tries not to lose more than one a round)

_____ takes a mulligan with the unreal pressure of not wanting to screw up twice in a row

_____ usually plays the white tees but is not above occasionally using the senior tee

_____ feels accomplishment when his score is not the highest in the group

Mark your score:
_____ / 20

If your score is over ten, you may have some duffer tendencies. Continue on and complete the next sections to determine if you have further duffer characteristics.

Duffer Ideals

____ Try to relax and enjoy each hole of golf you are able to play.

____ Make the best follow-up shots you can based on position, distance, hazards, and direction.

____ Don't overreact to a bad shot since the only cause is your error.

____ Record each shot since you only have to answer to yourself. ("To thine own self be true"—I heard that somewhere.)

____ Don't overreact to the pleasure of a par shot, birdie attempt, or on a super day, an eagle attempt.

____ Generously accept a gimme, pick it up, and when able, offer the same courtesy to playing partners.

____ Offer any knowledge of the hole from past experience to aid your playing group.

____ Courteously tell others that they may putt first since they are obviously farther away from the hole.

____ Observe and maintain a quiet decorum during each shot of the group.

____ Promptly tell the group scorer your tally at each hole and do not question others' tallies unless asked.

____ Provide needed GPS information to all group members.

____ Do not remind other players of their previous misfortunes on the current hole.

____ Do not make fun of other golfers no matter what they wear.

____ Honestly compliment other group members on a good golf shot.

____ Attempt to follow the hits of your group in order to aid them in finding their ball, thereby keeping a steady pace for the round.

____ Try not to cast a shadow by your stance or position of the cart into the area where a player is attempting a shot.

____ Mark your ball quickly on the green to assist play.

____ Avoid reminding a fellow golfer about water, hazards, out of bounds, etc., unless they inquire. The thought of these hazards might put undue (or excessive) pressure on the shot.

____ Quietly remind a player after an errant shot that they still have their mulligan.

____ After a round of golf, tally the lost balls, penalty strokes, and miscues that might have lowered your score to an acceptable number had they not occurred.

____ Always look forward to the next round.

____ Understand that you have the time between rounds to practice those shots you need help with, but you choose not to practice.

____ Realize that all those new clubs and gadgets you see advertised to help your score only help their profit.

____ Enjoy watching golf at an event or on television, especially when a professional golfer bogeys a hole, because you know that on a good day, from the white tee, you might be able to equal or beat that score.

____ Set realistic goals for a round of golf. Set a goal for the number of good shots you expect as well as the pars you hope to score.

____ Do not expect to win a bet with your group every time, but once in a while is encouraging.

__ Do not use the foot wedgie, to play as true to the game as possible.

____ Do not play in a divot, since you don't make any.

____ Realize that with every group of golfers, one player has to have the highest average score and handicap, and if it's you, try not to let it bother you. Try to improve, but also know you may have a few more handicap holes than the others and therefore more chances for a skin.

____ Understand that it is easy to make a bad shot; live with it and continue. Try to make up for it in small ways.

____ Set a goal to par every hole. But honestly realize you can't, so just give 100 percent on each shot and accept the outcome.

____ Try to remember how an error happened and concentrate a little harder at the next similar situation.

____ Realize it's a thinking game and that it is hard to fully focus on every stroke. Give it your best shot.

____ Try to remember you play best when your mind is focused in the present; don't worry about your score or life or trying to make that super shot—it will come naturally.

____ Treat other golfers the way you expect to be treated—except for the idiots.

____ Recall that two or more bad shots in a row sometimes occur; it does screw up a round. Try to let it go and move on. You can still win a skin and keep your high handicap.

____ Occasionally shoot a crappy round (defined as a high normal range score). You need to recall the few good shots.

____ Remember that you don't have to clean your clubs after every round; they have to earn that treat.

____ Approach each round and give each stroke your best attempt and move on to the next challenging stroke. Be creative, daring, sensible, or hope to be lucky.

____ Know you have the choice to play it safe or go for it in situations; do you feel lucky or do you still have a good round going?

Mark your score:

_____ / 40

If your score is above 20, you are continuing to enhance your duffer status.

Duffer Observations

____ Your club hitting distance shrinks with age.

____ You hate not seeing the ends of some of your shots; you follow the line they took.

____ You try not to overthink the game or a single shot.

____ When you have a positive attitude/feeling, you go for it.

____ If you have doubts, you play it safe.

____ It's a game, but you only want to be slightly challenged.

____ You play better later in the day.

____ Believe it or not, there are some days you just don't feel like playing.

____ So far, you haven't played one course so often that you "mastered" it.

____ You still don't like the self-induced pressure of the first tee.

____ You would like to play a round totally relaxed with no pressure.

____ You don't feel you have to keep changing and upgrading your equipment; you replace clubs as you break them.

____ You haven't justified the purchase of a golf cart yet, even though you live in a golfing community.

____ Your golf GPS does help in the selection of clubs.

____ You are able to clean both your club and ball as you retrieve them from the water hazard.

____ You have played some courses that are expensive, only to have the same duffer results.

____ You have had some lucky shots, but you would like to be more consistent.

____ You do appreciate a good shot, no matter who hits it.

____ You would like to play out of the sand confidently, but you don't practice.

____ You wish you could read a green.

____ You wish you could blank out a bad shot and start fresh on the next shot without impending doom.

____ You don't analyze your game; you know when you screw up and hope to avoid it next time.

____ There are some shots you feel very confident with and others you don't; it would be nice to be positive on all shots.

____ You will not knowingly hit into a group in front of you—although their slow play might encourage it.

____ You do not volunteer to drive the golf cart, since you would have to keep score and skins.

____ You try to visually follow the shot of your partners, if you can. Sometimes you lose sight of the ball.

____ You don't pass a bathroom without thinking about going to the restroom.

____ You don't spend undue time looking for a lost ball—you suck it up, drop a new ball, and take a penalty stroke.

____ If you whiff and no one sees, it still counts as a stroke.

____ If you land in a divot, and you never make a divot, a move out of the divot onto the grass is warranted.

____ Since you often putt from 25 yards off the green and in, you check for sprinkler heads around the green in your line to the hole and move your ball position to avoid the problem.

____ When you can't read a green, you go directly for the hole and then make your excuse.

____ If the result of your putt attempt is a gimme, you never question it.

____ Even in a group, you are playing against yourself.

____ When playing a course you've played before, you try to recall your best shots for good vibes.

____ If a sand trap is raked when you enter, you rake it on your exit—no matter how many shots you take.

____ Betting is nice if you win once in a while.

____ Since you don't take divots, maybe they should penalize those golfers who do. Perhaps a stroke for each divot sounds fair since it messes up the course.

____ You feel a little tense with the next shot when you have to clear the water.

____ You love the feel and distance of a "perfect" hit—even though it goes too far and enters the hazard.

Mark your score:

_____ / 40

Take a short break, grab a drink and a snack, and then continue on.

Duffer Experiences

____ Watching your putt on a perfect line stop 1 inch in front of the cup.

____ Observing your putt with the perfect line and speed until it hits the unrepaired ball impression and veers off.

____ Hitting the perfect shot off the fairway and realizing it may go farther than expected, right into the hazard.

____ You have a few excellent shots in a row (a rarity) and birdie the hole—as does your partner.

____ Hitting that perfect shot to the green, then noticing the slope as the ball rolls off.

____ The shot was perfect except for the tree; supposedly trees are 90 percent air.

____ Going to play the TPC course they use to play the Waste Management Phoenix Open and, with great expectation, getting to the par 3 stadium hole and realizing the stadium is only there for the tournament, then they take it down. Bummer.

____ Deciding to lay up, play it safe, and hit a terrible shot that ends up still unplayable.

____ Hate to be asked, "Did you see where my ball went?" and have no idea.

____ Having a great day on the tee until someone mentions it and you top the next drive.

____ You hit the iron shot you wanted, it feels perfect, you start to feel good about your game, and then the ball lands 1 foot short and runs down the slope away from the green.

____ You find your ball, but it is so close to the tree or bush that you can't make a shot.

____ Going into the clubhouse after a round knowing you have at least one good hole that should win a skin.

____ Enjoy playing a round away from the guys with no pressure; however, it doesn't always mean a better score.

____ Golf is a fun game until you screw up a round and wonder if it will be your worst score ever—you thought you already posted that one.

____ Enjoy each round as played and be pleased with one or two good holes.

____ Not getting depressed for 2 over your average on a round; it doesn't need to spoil your day—all you have to do is shoot 2 less next week to even it out.

____ Don't tell your golfing partner after you had a bad shot that you are going to the range later to work on it—because you know you won't.

____ "Nice shot" may not be what the hitter wants to hear based on his expectations.

____ After a rotten shot, hearing "that should be an easy up and down" only puts more pressure on the shot.

____ Going to a difficult course that you have played before, which has many hazards, and wondering if you will lose more balls than last time.

____ Trying to convince yourself that your next shot won't be affected by the slow play and continuous waiting for the group in front of you.

____ While addressing your second shot, you are told by your partner "maybe you should wait, they may be too close"—a certain prelude to a miss hit.

____ While waiting at the tee, you observe that the first three of the foursome have had great shots, now it's your turn.

____ The quasi-good feeling after hitting the shot well, albeit 10 yards farther than needed.

____ The good/bad feeling of hitting a really good shot, better than usual, that lands on the green—however, the foursome in front of you has not finished yet.

____ Hearing "you have honors" and realizing you need a good drive.

____ The good feeling you have standing on the green after 2 decent shots but then looking back to the tee and seeing that they are waiting for you to clear the green so they can hit.

____ The irritating feeling when, after a decent hit, the ball rolls through the fairway and nestles in an animal burrow or water furrow, rendering it unplayable.

____ While waiting in the fairway to take your second shot, the drive from the group behind you rolls 10 feet past you, and you wrestle with the urge to run the cart over the ball or to tee it up and hit it back toward the tee box.

____ The disappointment of not seeing the cart girl when you really need a snack.

____ The unpleasant wait to hit your next shot that occurs when you have hit your previous shot to the center of the next fairway.

____ The undue pressure you feel to play that errant shot from the next fairway back to your fairway. Are they watching?

____ The stressful feeling you get after you drop your ball in the drop zone behind the water hazard and proceed to hit the next shot into the same hazard.

____ The uneasy feeling that turns to undue pressure as you try to hit from the sand trap only intensified by the second, third, or maybe fourth shot to get out.

____ The downside of an additional hour tee time delay due to weather.

____ The feeling of executing the perfect lay up shot only diminished by the next shot into the hazard.

____ The unwillingness to give up on a round of golf due to driving rain, perhaps even accented by lightning. This lessens with age.

____ The misfortune of playing behind a foursome of "professionals" who take mega time to contemplate each shot.

____ The excellent drive down the center of the fairway as the rest of your group scatters their drives.

____ The chip from off the green that works its way into the hole.

____ The putt you drained for par from an amazing distance.

____ From that impossible lie, somehow you hit the ball onto the green.

____ Your foursome bet closest to the pin on a par 3, and it was your ball.

____ The good feeling when another golfer in your group goes up to the longest drive on the hole thinking it was their hit—then realizes it was yours.

____ You make a par and none of your group did.

____ That special feeling as you watch your ball skip over the water hazard to land safely on the other side.

____ You have a good hole and win a bet from the group.

____ After winning honors for the next hole, you actually hit a quality drive on that hole.

____ Knowing your play on that hole helped the team score, but telling them not to expect much more.

____ You birdie a hole.

____ You have a shot at an eagle and you have to settle for a birdie.

____ You drive a par 3 and end up less than one foot from the cup.

____ Watching that perfect shot clear the hazard and land in a safe area.

____ Finding the restroom when you really need it.

____ You record one of your lowest rounds ever.

____ Matching your playing partner shot for shot on a hole.

____ You execute a perfect sand save and know how lucky you are.

____ Telling your playing partner how you intend to play the next shot and then making it (a rarity).

____ You end up with a decent score even though you had a couple 8s.

Mark your score:

_____ / 60

Time to refill that drink, hold the snack, and then continue on.

Duffer Expressions

Check those in your current usage.

____ Fore

____ Turn! Turn!

____ Roll . . . keep rolling

____ Hit the cart path

____ Bounce left (or right)

____ Go the other way

____ Topped it

____ Off the toe

____ Off the heel

____ I still have my mulligan

____ Do you think I can find it?

____ Get through it

____ Is that out of bounds?

____ Should I hit a provisional?

____ You "*@#!&#" ball

____ Wrong club

____ Did you see where it landed?

____ Did it go into the backyard?

____ Do you have a ball retriever?

____ How far is the hazard?

____ The green is wide open

____ My game is a little "off" today

____ Damn

____ I lost it

____ Got under it

____ Skyed it

____ Did it clear the Ladies Tee?

____ Do you have a GPS?

____ Did it clear the trap?

____ Do you think I should hit?

____ I can't hit that far

____ Did you see it come out from the tree?

____ I'm going to go for it

____ How far do you think it is?

____ What did you use?

____ It should be around here

____ Is there a trap on the other side too?

____ Where's the drop zone?

____ Keep going

____ Stop! Stop! Stop!

____ Could have hit it lighter (or stronger)

____ Good line

____ That's playable

____ What tree?

____ I could play it safe

____ I think I can hit it

____ It was supposed to come off the hill

____ Is it in the other fairway?

____ Is that my ball or yours?

____ Oh, so close

____ Bite! Bite!

____ Almost

____ It should break left (or right)

____ I thought it would break

____ Would you mark your ball?

____ Would you tend the pin?

____ Response to "that's a gimme" is thank you

____ Did it roll off the green?

____ I think I can knock it out of there

____ The fairway is wide open

_____/ 60

Record your scores below:

Duffer Description   _____/ 20

Duffer Ideals   _____/ 40

Duffer Observations_____/ 40

Duffer Experiences _____/ 60

Duffer Expressions _____/ 60

    Total   _____/220

Now is the time of reckoning.

If your total score exceeds 110, you exhibit some duffer tendencies. The higher your score, the more you approach joining me as the complete duffer.

Based on your total, you could go back to some of the sections and erase some of your responses to lower your score, but since a golf pencil doesn't have an eraser, you might have to find another pencil.

Relax now, the hard part is over. Top up that drink and continue on to the next section to participate in a duffer round of golf.

SECTION 3

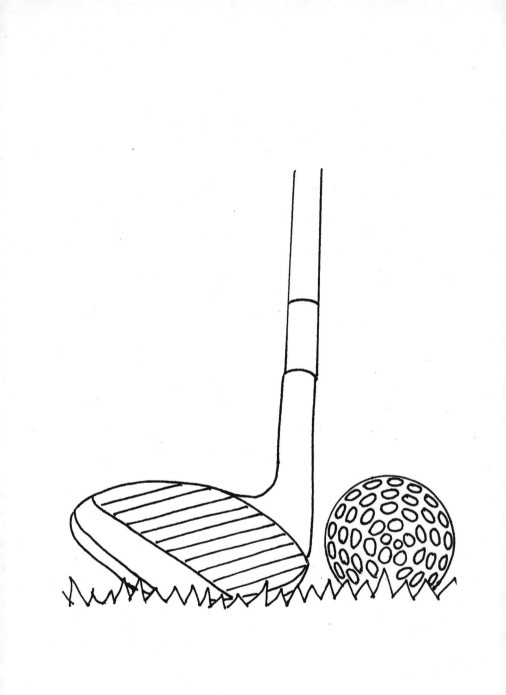

Preface

For my book, you would think I would pick one of my best rounds to describe in detail. Instead, I just selected the next course I was going to play and hoped for a good round.

The day was a typical Arizona day, bright and sunny, temperature in the 80s. We were able to tee off about fifteen minutes early from our 10:30 tee time. My playing partner had a handicap of one better than mine, so it should have been a nice round with no pressure. We played the white tees on this round and our pace of play was unaffected by the group in front. The cart girl even showed up when needed.

Grab your pencil, get your drink, sit back, and join me on my round of duffer golf. You may follow my play by connecting the dots of my shots on each hole. Now turn the page and step up to the first tee.

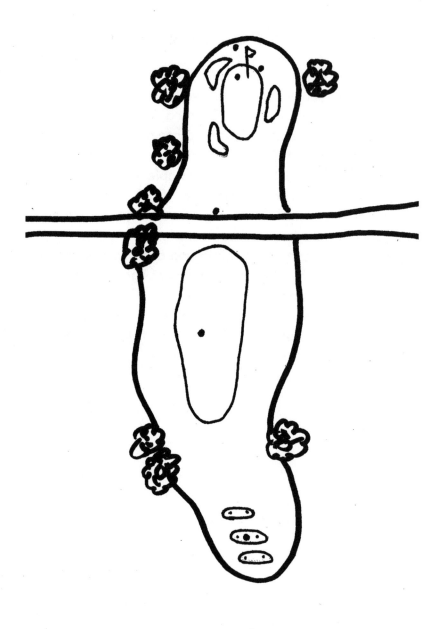

Hole 1 384 Yards Par 4

1 Good start with driver down the center of the fairway about 210 yards.

2 Second shot was poorly struck with 9 metal hybrid traveling about 100 yards and just cleared the water hazard by one foot.

3 Using chipper, hit the ball about 7 yards over the back of the green.

4 Using chipper again, a soft hit short to back of the green about 20 feet from pin.

5 Putt to hole and the ball stops about 18 inches from cup.

6 Putt conceded. (Gimme)

Score 6   Good hits 2

Hole 2 348 Yards Par 4

1 The drive was pulled left, hit a tree, and dropped to the fairway side about 110 yards.
2 Using the 3 metal wood, advanced the ball about 180 yards to the right side.
3 Using the chipper, avoided the sand trap and advanced to the front edge of the green about 15 feet from cup.
4 Strong putt and the ball ran past the hole by 3 feet.
5 Putted into cup.

Score 5   Good hits 1

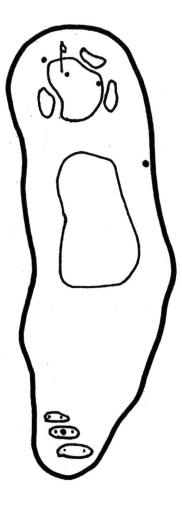

Hole 3 177 Yards Par 3

1 With a 5 fairway hybrid, hit the right of the fairway about 160 yards.
2 Using chipper, sent the ball across the green rolling 2 yards off the back side.
3 Chipper again, a little hard, and the ball rolled 12 feet past the hole.
4 Putted to within 1 foot.
5 Putt conceded. (Gimme)

Score 5   Good hits 0

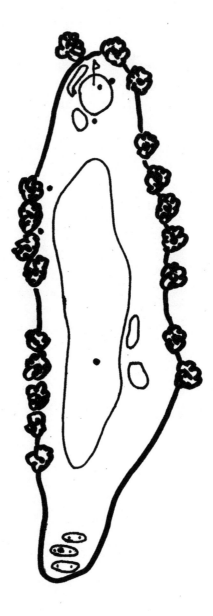

Hole 4 464 Yards Par 4

1 Good drive down the center about 200 yards.
2 Using a 3 metal wood, the ball travelled about 170 yards to the left in a tree line.
3 Using a 7 iron and trying to keep it low, lofted it into the trees and it landed about 30 yards ahead.
4 Using chipper, topped it and it travelled about 50 yards to front of green.
5 Using putter, hit it firmly past the hole to the back of the green.
6 Putted to about 3 feet from cup.
7 Putted into hole.

Score 7   **Good hits 1**

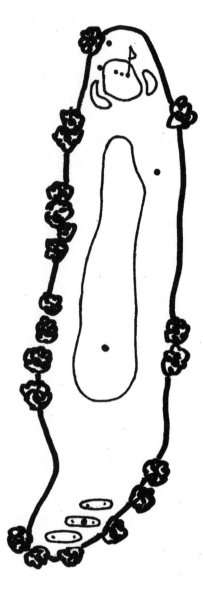

Hole 5 461 Yards Par 5

1 A longer drive down center about 220 yards.
2 Using 3 metal wood, ball travelled about 170 yards down the right side of the fairway.
3 Using a pitching wedge, powered a shot 20 yards over the green.
4 Using chipper, the ball reached the back edge of the green about 25 feet from cup.
5 Putted a little short to 6 feet from hole.
6 Putted to about 6 inches from hole.
7 Putt conceded. (Gimme)

Score 7   Good hits 1

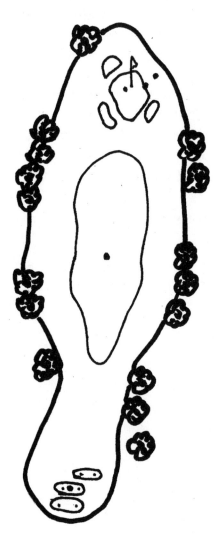

Hole 6 371 Yards Par 4

1 Good drive about 215 yards down the center.
2 Using 3 metal wood, crushed the ball about 180 yards over the green to the back right rough and 10 yards from the green.
3 Chipper from thick grass, ball advanced to edge of green about 10 feet from hole.
4 Putted to about 1 foot.
5 Putt conceded. (Gimme)

Score 5   Good hits 2

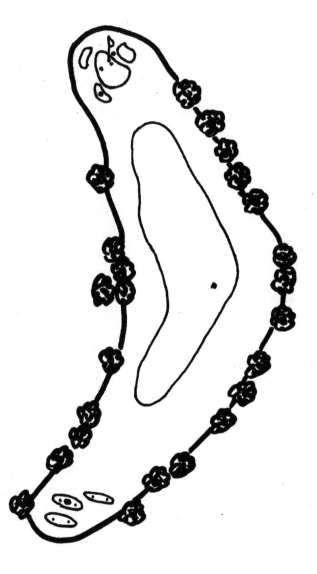

Hole 7 372 Yards Par 4

1 Nice drive to center about 225 yards.
2 Using 7 metal wood, found the sand trap on the left of the green.
3 A firm sand wedge put the ball over the green.
4 From off the green, putted to about 5 feet from the hole.
5 Putted to about 2 inches from the cup.
6 Putt conceded. (Gimme)

Score 6   Good hits 1

Hole 8 160 yards Par 3

1 Using a 5 iron, the ball landed in rough on left side of fairway about 10 yards from green.
2 Using the chipper, the ball landed at the front edge of the green about 25 feet from cup.
3 Mishit putt to about 7 feet from the hole.
4 Putted to a distance of 1 foot from hole.
5 Putt conceded. (Gimme)

Score 5   Good hits 0

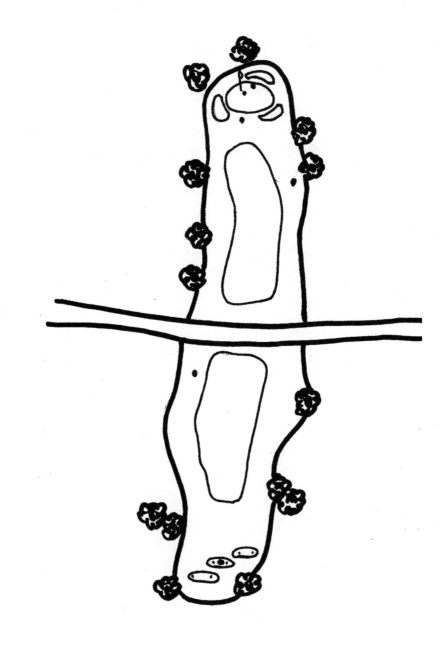

Hole 9 423 Yards Par 5

1 Good drive about 190 yards down the left side of fairway.
2 Using 3 metal, hit the ball to the right side of the fairway about 170 yards.
3 Using pitching wedge, hit a soft shot to front apron about 20 feet from pin.
4 Putted firmly past the hole about 7 feet.
5 Putted to about 6 inches.
6 Putt conceded. (Gimme)

Score 6   Good hits 2

FRONT NINE TOTAL: 52

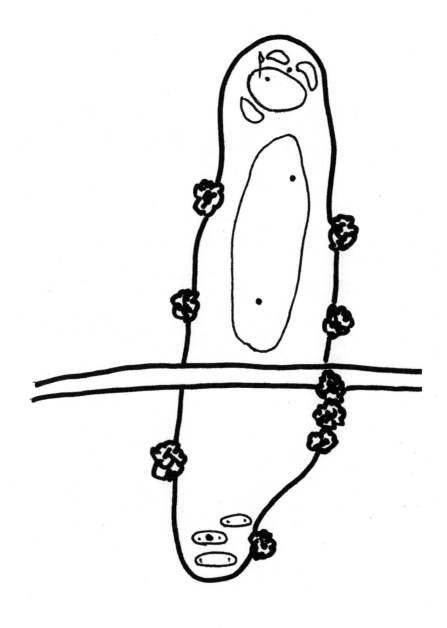

Hole 10 440 Yards Par 4

1 A good drive down the center about 200 yards.
2 Using a 3 metal wood, the ball travelled about 160 yards down the fairway.
3 Using a 9 iron, hit a shot to just off the right back side of the green.
4 Using a chipper, hit the ball to about 2 feet from the hole.
5 Putted into hole.

Score 5   Good hits 3

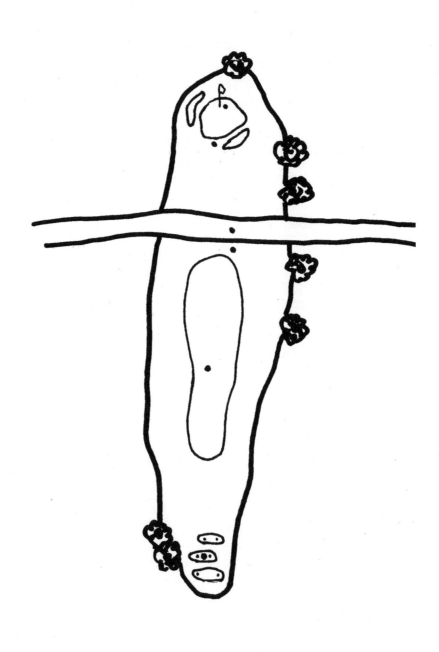

Hole 11 365 Yards Par 4

1 Nice drive down the center about 180 yards.
2 Using 3 metal wood, topped the ball as a low liner that ran up and into the creek about 140 yards. (minus 1 ball)
3 Dropped a ball.
4 Using a sand wedge, pitched to front of green about 30 feet from cup.
5 Putted to about 10 inches from hole.
6 Putt conceded. (Gimme)

Score 6   Good hits 1

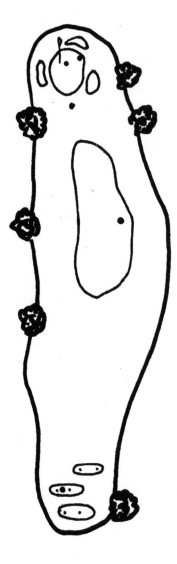

Hole 12 300 Yards Par 4

1 Short drive of 175 yards.
2 Using a 7 iron, hit to about 10 yards off front of green.
3 Using chipper, hit the ball firmly to back edge of green about 15 feet from cup.
4 Putted to about 2 feet from hole.
5 Putted in.

Score 5   **Good hits 0**

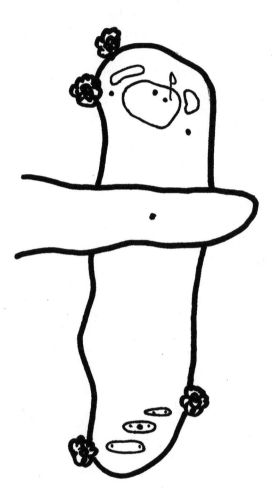

Hole 13 112 Yards Par 3

1 Using 9 iron, hit a high short shot into the water. (minus 1 ball)

Mulligan
1 Using 8 iron, hit to right side of the fairway about 110 yards.
2 Using chipper, ball rolled past back side of green about 5 yards.
3 Putted to about 6 feet from hole.
4 Putted to about 6 inches from hole.
5 Putt conceded. (Gimme)

Score 5   Good hits 0

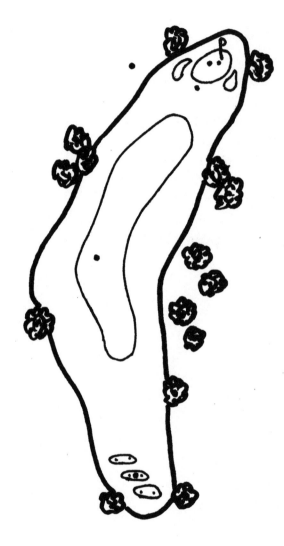

Hole 14 312 Yards Par 4

1 Good drive down the center about 200 yards.
2 Using 9 iron, pulled shot left and wide of fairway by about 20 yards.
3 Using chipper, hit to front apron of green about 35 feet from hole.
4 Putted lightly to about 10 feet from hole.
5 Putted to 8 inches from cup.
6 Putt conceded. (Gimme)

Score 6   **Good hits 1**

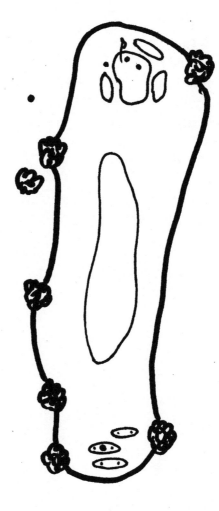

Hole 15 195 Yards Par 3

1 Using 3 metal wood, hit about 180 yards left of green by about 30 yards.
2 Using sand wedge, pitched to about 6 feet from green near sand trap.
3 Putted firmly and ball ran past hole about 7 feet.
4 Putted to about 1 foot from cup.
5 Putt conceded. (Gimme)

Score 5   **Good hits 0**

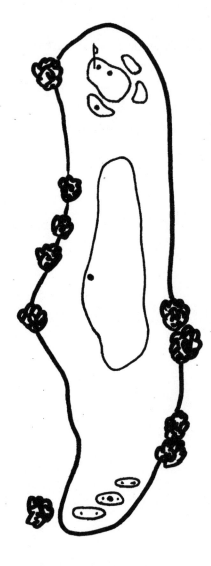

Hole 16 345 Yards Par 4

1 Good drive down left side of fairway about 210 yards.
2 Using 9 metal wood, hit well but ended up in left sand trap.
3 Using sand wedge, hit ball to about 6 feet from hole.
4 Putted to about 4 inches away.
5 Putt conceded. (Gimme)

Score 5   Good hits 1

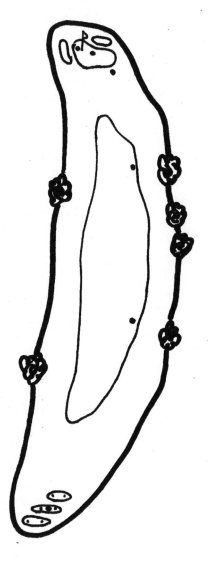

Hole 17 468 Yards Par 5

1 Nice drive down center about 205 yards.
2 Using 3 metal wood, hit a nice shot down the right side of the fairway about 170 yards.
3 Using a 9 iron, hit to right front apron of the green about 40 feet from pin.
4 Putted to about 5 feet from cup.
5 Putted to about 1 foot past hole.
6 Putt conceded. (Gimme)

Score 6   Good hits 2

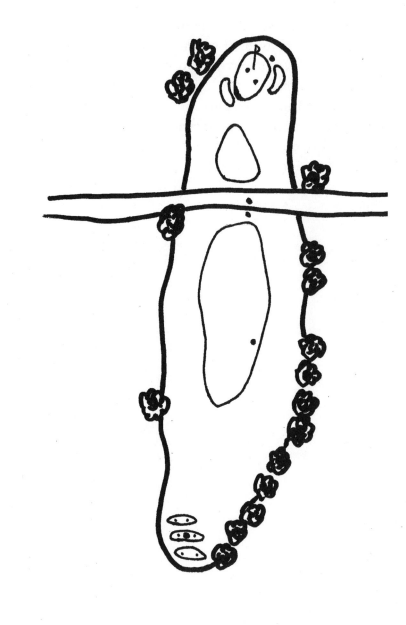

Hole 18 481 Yards Par 5

1 Final drive down center about 200 yards.
2 Using 5 metal wood, trying to lay up in front of stream, hit hard and well, and ball rolled into hazard. (minus 1 ball)
3 Dropped ball.
4 Using 8 iron, hit to back right side off the green.
5 Misread putt and ball took break to about 10 feet from the cup.
6 Putted to about 2 feet from cup.
7 Putted in hole.

Score 7   Good hits 1

This round: 50 and 52, for 102
3 Lost balls
20 Good hits

13 Gimmes

Review

If after you examined this round of golf you feel you could do better, remember it wasn't one of my better days. Without three water balls, I would have broken 100. Of nine putts that ended up less than 1 foot from the cup, if I could have made half, I would be at 95, not counting my 5 mishits. But as we know, you get what you get.

In reviewing the round, I need to be better with my chipper. Will I work at it? I'll think about it. Maybe this was just a bad day with it. As you know, sometimes the driver works well and nothing else, sometimes it's another club, and sometimes a few things just work together. There is always the next round. I suppose if you wanted a really good score, you could play miniature golf.

FYI: The next round I played, two days later and on a different course, I had a different outcome. The score was 10 strokes less with 5 pars but also included two holes of 7 and two holes of 8, plus one lost ball. It could have been a real good round, but the duffer surfaced.

You can tell how poorly your round is going if too often, you are the last of the group to tee off, since you had the highest score on the previous hole—or, if you are consistently the first to putt on the greens, since you are the farthest away from the hole. Realize that once in a while you are the first to tee off. Do you really want the pressure? Or is it better to watch the other three players hit their shots before you hit your drive? A duffer's dilemma.

SECTION 4

- ➢ Duffing Epilogue
- ➢ Duffing Impressions
- ➢ Duffing Good Day

Duffing Epilogue

If, after reading my book, you find that you have some duffer tendencies, it's not the end of the world. My intention was to reassure readers that being a duffer is not a bad thing. I try to present the duffer as a student of the game learning and developing skills as he or she plays. The experience is made more enjoyable by the occasional great shot (glimpse of perfection) that shows what is possible to attain.

Although I never have come close to the pin again on the hole I aced years ago, I do appreciate my luck that day. So enjoy your good shots and remember them; they keep you coming back. Remember, hope springs eternal.

Duffing Impressions

Just when you think you're finished writing, you get thoughts of more things.

You wonder if there is a definition or any such thing as a perfect round in golf. Would it be all birdies or should it include an eagle, double eagle, or even one or two holes in one?

After you set goals for each round and begin to achieve them, realize there are rounds that are occasional setbacks, but continue on.

Be sure to enjoy each round. Take pleasure in the good shots, and forget the bad ones. Hopefully you will reach the day when you have more good than bad shots. Each round is a test—you against the course.

Once in a while you play in bad weather. Since you recall that a bad day on the golf course is better than a good day at work, you enjoy it. Plus, you have a possible excuse for a bad round. Unfortunately, as you get older, rain and cold stop the round sooner.

When you approach the first tee, it's nice to see a course that has senior tees, and you choose the white ones.

You hate to drive by a golf course when you have free time, and when you're on the course you don't really care what time it is.

Usually the bad round of golf is forgotten by the time you get home, the good round is savored a bit longer, and the good hits keep you coming back.

Sometimes you experience the game as a nature walk where you encounter a soaring hawk, ducks and birds (that approach the cart for a snack), rabbits, groundhogs, coyotes, deer, and even notice the fish (while looking for your ball).

You play the game for relaxation, enjoyment, friendship, and accomplishment, plus a few good holes. You even wish your playing partners good luck but not too much.

It's not a disgrace to be a duffer. As a happy duffer, you know your skills and limitations and try to improve your game each time out.

Finishing this book may allow me more time for improvement on the course. One day I may be able to shoot my age, hopefully sooner than later. Presently at age 66, it would take me 18 years to match my best score of 84, and some 30+ years to match my current scores. To attain this goal sooner would take some work, and you know my thoughts on work.

I tried to make a phrase from the letters of

D – Dreaming the
U – ultimate
F – fairway
F – fantasy
E – every
R – round

Duffing Good Day

I had finished this book and was letting the pages just sit for a little while. During that time I had played three rounds of my usual golf.

I was in charge of scheduling the next round of golf for my group, and I chose to go back to the course in my book.

(I also had a free round at the course, which may have affected my choice.)

I scored a lackluster 55 on the front nine and made the turn for the back nine with the eternal hope of a fresh start while forgetting the front nine. Through the first three holes, I found myself at 5 over par. Then came the short #13 par 3 over water (where I had placed many shots). I stroked well, the ball landed softly on the green, and I was able to par the hole. At the next hole, #14 par 4, my second shot found the sand trap to the right of the green. With my sand wedge, and not much confidence, I was able to hit the perfect chip that went straight into the cup for a birdie. I had never before holed any shot out of the sand, let alone for a birdie! I moved on to #15 par 3, 195 yards with sand traps left, right, and back. Using my 3 metal wood, I hit one of the best shots, if not the best, that I have ever struck. As the ball sailed straight toward the flag, it bounced in front of the green and rolled into the cup. A hole in one, with witnesses. (Two of whom also witnessed my first ace.) I did repeatedly say "thank you" very loudly many times after retrieving the ball from the hole.

This was the best series of three holes I ever played or hoped to play.

One of my playing partners had been making fun of the pinkish ball I was playing. He stopped doing that.

After teeing off on the next hole, I retired the hole-in-one ball so I wouldn't lose it.

I proceeded to finish and carded a 42, one of my better outings.

A great day; it doesn't get much better than this. Sometimes it pays to be just plain lucky.

My parting advice for all you duffers is to keep at it. Your duffing good day is coming. Only don't do better than I did, or I'll have to read your book.

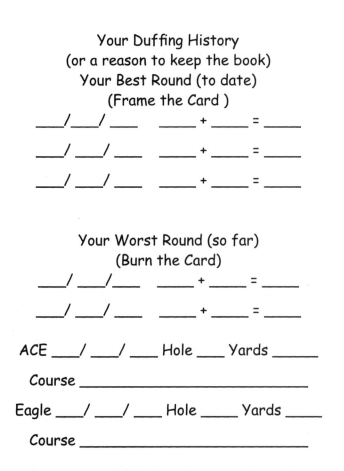

Your Duffing History
(or a reason to keep the book)
Your Best Round (to date)
(Frame the Card)

___/___/___   ___ + ___ = ___

___/ ___/ ___   ___ + ___ = ___

___/ ___/ ___   ___ + ___ = ___

Your Worst Round (so far)
(Burn the Card)

___/ ___/___   ___ + ___ = ___

___/ ___/ ___   ___ + ___ = ___

ACE ___/ ___/ ___ Hole ___ Yards _____

Course _____

Eagle ___/ ___/ ___ Hole ____ Yards ____

Course _____

Best series of holes

Highest number of birdies in a round _____

Most gimmes in a round _____ _____ _____

Most lost balls in a round _____ _____ _____

(Do they sell ball insurance?)

Number of different courses played _____

Favorite Courses

_____

_____

Courses that you don't like (they suck)

_____

_____

Memorable Shots

Your Duffing Good Day Comments